ANCHORED

THE DISCIPLINE TO STOP DRIFTING.

LUCAS SKROBOT

www.LucasSkrobot.com

Designed and Typeset in USA;

Printed and bound in USA;

ISBN-13: 9781696567626

for my wife who never gives up
my children who are always growing
and for every dreamer and creator
striving to be fruitful and effective

Contents

INTRODUCTION

Change of Culture

It was the summer of 2008. I was 22 years young. I graduated from University of Colorado, Denver, and entered the glorious world of "adulthood". Nothing but a magical land full of golden opportunities lay ahead of me. And, the best part of it all, I had absolutely not the slightest clue what I was doing.

I lacked structure. I lacked direction. I had far too much time at my disposal. More than anything I wanted to be effective with my life. I wanted to be fruitful. Whether I was seen or unseen, I yearned to be squeezing the most out of every minute of the day.

As I set out, as an overly zealous youth, I unknowingly created a formula to measure my effectiveness and my fruitfulness. I came to believe that if I was busy then

I was effective. After all—important people seem to be consistently busy.

Western Culture idolizes busyness. If you don't believe me ask a few friends what they have been up to. They will probably answer with, "Oh man, I've been so busy. Crazy." We give this rote answer all the time. I was the same way.

I had to feel busy to feel effective. I had a never-ending to-do list. I was always too busy to hang out with friends because I had some task that needed to be completed to remain busy and feel effective.

If I had down time, I would pull out my to-do list. If I had nothing to do I would create a task for myself. I was sure my hard, diligent work was making me successful and significant. Yet, I would go to bed every night in shame feeling as if I didn't do enough.

Then something dynamically changed. All my busy work and narrow focus paid off with an opportunity for adventure. My wife and six-month-old son boarded a plane and we moved our entire life to the Middle East to pursue a business opportunity and adventure of a life time.

As I embarked on this adventure, I realized, on a shallow intellectual level, Middle Eastern Culture was different from Western Culture. But I didn't realize Middle Eastern Culture would impact me on such a deep level.

In the West, important people are busy. Important people walk fast, they are glued to their phones, their schedules are booked, they have constant conference calls, emails, and events.

In the East, important people walk slow, and seem to never have anything to do other than chat the night away. Life moves slowly. People of honor are not dictated by time—and servants hurry around.

Encountering this new culture challenged all my presupposition on effectiveness and fruitfulness. No longer could I make to-do lists and pound them out in a few hours— everything takes 10 times longer in the East than in the developed Western World. I still made my to-do lists to feel effective, but when my task was to practice Arabic and instead of practice I had to wait a few hours for a friend to show up, life became frustrating. Or, if he did show up, frustration could quickly set in when language capabilities were exhausted and both parties resorted to long spells of silence. After all—I needed to be busy advancing my career, and learning what little language I could. And sitting in silence certainly wasn't advancing my life.

Life slowed down. We expected life to be full of excitement and adventure, but instead it sapped us of all energy, motivation, and strength.

I realized my presupposition of busyness and effectiveness might not be sound. My meter of fruitfulness and effectiveness was wrong.

I started searching, reading, praying, thinking, and writing. Change was needed. But it was frightening to let go of my western busy culture. It was difficult to give up my algorithm of effectiveness and success.

What if I was wrong about being wrong? What if I let go of my relentless work mentality, which was the driving force that got us on this adventure in the first place, and ended up failing? What if I became common and forgettable?

In the following pages you will read about my small, yet significant, discoveries that transformed and is transforming my life. It has changed the way I think, live, work, and measure my life.

I wish I could tell you I no longer struggle with feelings of ineffectiveness. I still do. But I now have an array of tools to help battle the temptation of reentering the maddening busyness of the west. I have a new lens by which I approach life, weigh options, and make decisions.

It is my hope that this book provides you with a new perspective to becoming effective. I hope these perspectives free you to walk into your purpose in new and greater measures.

CHAPTER ONE

Anchored is Mundane

As a kid growing up in Papua New Guinea, I loved to make treasure maps, burning the edges and browning the paper so they would appear old. I thought my little maps were so cool. I felt adventurous using them to search for treasure. I also felt conflicted with the depressing knowledge that the maps weren't real and that the treasure for which I was "searching" did not exist.

I wished more than anything that I could go on a real adventure through the jungles to find a real hidden treasure. My friends and I even took all the cash we had, traded it in for small change, and then filled a wooden chest, pretending we were rich. We longed for adventure, a chance to overcome adversity against all odds. Even now, when I go outdoors in the jungle, I transform into another person. The boy who grew up wandering the mountainsides of Papua New Guinea comes out, and I'm back on the trail, searching for adventure.

We all yearn for adventure, the feeling that something great might happen at any moment. Even the most fearful people who stay at home and live vicariously through television, the Internet, or social media, desire to live on the edge. Otherwise they wouldn't be trying to fill the void in their lives with entertainment. Even those crushed by failure, disappointment, loss, and depression; beneath it all is a desire to live free of fear and full of adventure. We were created to explore, to discover, to learn.

To help feed this desire, we go on weekend adventures, vacations to exotic destinations, or guided safaris, because these experiences allow us to encounter risk safely. After a few days, weeks, or hours, we return home feeling like heroes, having had a taste of action and adventure. Such experiences give us a shot of adrenalin. We feel as though we have risked much. But although the feeling is intense, it fades quickly. Months pass, and we begin looking for another taste, because we have been deceived into thinking the short-term adrenaline high of adventure equates to living a great life. The truth is, we are actually avoiding greatness. Real adventure, real greatness, is found through labor over decades. Living adventurously happens when we live obediently through the mundane.

If I'm honest with myself, the desire for adventure, and yearning to live on the edge and travel the world was a major driver in our journey overseas. We expected to be enthralled with the Arab culture. We envisioned picking up the language overnight, spending long hours laughing and sharing stories with new friends, and while basking in new found success.

If only achieving your dreams in a foreign context were that simple. Instead, I spent time driving around tirelessly in search for black beans for dinner, waiting in long lines at border crossings, and crisscrossing the nation to different governmental offices to get the right stamps in the right order on our marriage certificate to prove we are married. We expected to have unbelievable stories every week, but all we had to show for our time was unintelligible scribbles of Arabic grammar structures, and nervous breakdowns from running to every government office in the country in an attempt to register a company. Life was boring. Many times, in despair, we asked, "What on earth are we doing here? We are wasting our lives." The exciting, brave, "life on the edge" was far from glamorous. It was lonely, and boring. Our perception of the path to success was deeply skewed. As I started recognizing wrong paradigms I started to notice a similar pattern in other stories as well.

If we take a close look at some of our most celebrated figures in real life and fiction, we find our perception of their lives is quite skewed from the reality of their struggle. Take Tolkien's *The Lord of the Rings*, for example. The three-book trilogy takes place over a timespan of almost three years. Frodo and Sam spend, over those three year, 185 days walking,[1] during which they cover a distance of 1,779 miles (2,970 km).[2] They spend most of their time hiking over mountains, through caves, and across plains, setting up and taking down camp, day after day. During their 185 days of walking, only 37 noteworthy events occurred.[3] After the first month, they are most likely bored, tired, and close to giving up. It wasn't anything like the adventure they thought it would be. They were sleeping in the rain, hungry, eating bland food, and running from people—and creatures—who wanted to kill them. They walked for miles without seeing a soul, wondering if they would ever arrive at their destination or if they would survive to return home. Sure, there were moments of excitement or adventure, but in no way was the adventure fun or enjoyable. When it wasn't deadly boring, it was plain deadly. Ironically, we still find ourselves wishing our lives were as exciting as Sam and Frodo's. The same goes when we think about historical characters.

The Prophet Noah

The story of the Noah the Prophet is shared by Judaism, Christianity, and Islam. The story of Noah and a great flood is also found in the folk history of many other cultures.

Noah built a huge boat, believing God would destroy the earth through a flood. He herded the animals onto the boat, the rain came, and Noah and his family are saved to repopulate the earth. What an incredible adventure.

Or was it?

The story of the flood is so dramatic that it's easy to forget how boring and uneventful Noah's life was up to, and even after, he received that fateful word from God.

"Noah, this is God."

"Yes?"

"I'm going to kill everyone, build a boat."

"Okay. How?"

"I'm glad you asked. Here are the dimensions, put a roof on it. Oh, and I'm promoting you to executive zookeeper and food gatherer. Good luck."

"Oh . . . uh . . . "

After a hundred years of taunting and ridicule by friends, the ark is finished. The animals and Noah's family pile inside. It rains for forty days. The earth flooded for forty more days. They sit on the ark feeding the animals for another 150 days because the earth was still covered by water. The ark finally hits a mountain, and they sit for another forty days waiting for the water to subside. For twenty-one more days, they wait and send out birds in search of dry land. Finally, Noah steps off the ark to see if the land is dry and then continues to wait another two months before disembarking. All in all, Noah and his family sat on the boat for 370 incredibly boring days.

Let's recap. The Prophet Noah lives five hundred years in obscurity, gets mocked as he builds a big boat for a hundred years without any sign of rain, and then spends over a year locked up inside with his family and hundreds of smelly animals. He lives for another 350 years with no stories worth telling, apart from getting drunk, being exposed, and then getting laughed at by his son Ham. Despite such momentary lapses, Noah was a hero, a great man of God, faithful and steadfast. But an adventurer? Hardly.

Unfortunately, our inaccurate view of people like Frodo, Noah and a host of other historical and fictional characters distort our view of adventure. We embark on our adventures of obedience, full of excitement. Then the mundaneness of everyday life kicks in, and we begin to question whether we are truly on the right path. We become deceived into believing we are no longer doing great things.

Bored, we start searching for a new adventure, the next sense of calling—the next thing that stirs our emotions. Instead of sticking around for the entire game, we want to rush straight to the highlight reel. We change course—missing out on the real adventure that was to come if we had been able to endure. As a result, we fail to accomplish anything of lasting value.

We must find value in the mundane. The mundane is the process that takes us from point A to point B. The mundane is the catalyst that creates motion and growth. Faith and grit is tested in the mundane. In the mundane, we grow and are pruned. Once we reach point B, "The next exciting moment," we might think to ourselves "Yes, finally, I've been waiting for this moment. I've grown. I've achieved. I've progressed." Yet, progress isn't about arrival. Progress occurs through imperceptible movements during the monotonous seasons. The "event" is only a mile marker, a blip on the screen informing you the mundane is working.

If you were to decide to climb Mt. Everest, what would be most important part of achieving that goal? Would it be the final step taken upon reaching the summit? That would be a great moment, however, it would merely be the fulfillment of your hard work. It is not your perseverance over the last hundred meters that makes you great but the endurance, sacrifice, and discipline over the years leading up to that final moment. Climbing Everest does not begin when you land in Nepal or arrive at basecamp. You start climbing Everest the day you start training. Each training session might feel insignificant, but each session builds upon the next, creating unquantifiable worth over time.

Each moment is infinitely small, but they all add up to seconds, and seconds add up to a lifetime. In the same manner, great achievements are composed of millions of moments that are stewarded correctly. It doesn't matter if the achievement is learning to play guitar or winning an Oscar. Any achievement starts with small, seemingly insignificant steps and minute decisions. Do not despise the days of small beginnings. The small beginnings are far more significant than the pinnacles of success, just as the foundation of a skyscraper is far more critical to its longevity than the final golden spire.

The simple power of faithfulness through the mundane will bring moments of adrenaline, breaking you through to achieve the goals towards which you have been laboring. If you live for the completion of goals, however, you will find disappointment and despair right when you expect to find your greatest joy and ecstasy. It is not the achievement, the adventure, or the moment of arrival that builds our character but the long road of endurance over decades.

Suffering, steadfastness through the monotonous grind of life produces character, a character of overcoming. The ability to overcome through pure grit and stubbornness produces a wild-eyed hope. This hope gives life to our dreams.

It births passion in every word we speak. This hope breathes life into all who hear its voice. The hope of all things working together for our good empowers us through the mundane struggles of life.

Mundane tasks set us up for greatness. Our character is built in the mundane so that when the big moments come, we're mature enough to handle it. Without such a vision, we will abandon the refining fire, hammering, and endless friction applied to our lives, which forges us into the sharp swords of determination, empowering us to overcome.

Commitment Is Radical

We need to stop being radical and start being committed. Commitment and dedication to the fundamentals will set us apart in the long run—and even in the short term. The newfangled thing, the revolutionary breakthrough, the new discovery, or next new, great proven method will land you in the gutter. Good ol' boring hard work and commitment to the fundaments will land you as a true outlier long after all your big talking friends have fallen out of the race.

We live in an always progressing and cutting-edge culture. We strive to stand out from the crowd and do something brave, new, and noteworthy. Innovation is good. So is creating or doing something that is unique and important enough for people to pause and take notice. We need to continue to innovate, grow, improve, and revolutionize the world. We cannot afford to live in the status quo, because it will make us complacent. No one wants to be ordinary. We all desire to be the on the cutting edge of our field. We want to stand out, be noticed, extraordinary, which is great.

The catch is, everyone else is striving to stand out, too. As a result, it's easy for your efforts to distinguish yourself to become nothing but white noise, easily tuned out. The few people who do pull ahead seem to, "get lucky." They are in the right place at the right time. After all, everyone has twenty-four hours in his or her day, and everyone is working hard to be extreme. Therefore, some people must get lucky and others not, right?

This is not the case. Don't fall prey to fatalism, which leads to hopelessness. If fate rules the world, then we might as well sit around waiting for Lady Luck to come calling. I don't believe in luck. I believe in divine appointment, divine favor, and positioning ourselves to steward the opportunities that come our way.

In general, the mindset of those who are bursting in an attempt to be cutting edge stems from a get-rich-quick mentality, and chasing the latest fads hoping to hit it big. They have the subtle, underlying hope that extremism will cause people to take notice, flinging open the doors of opportunity. This mindset is built around a framework constructed of half-truths from individuals who seem to have come out of nowhere, caught a lucky break, and happened upon success overnight. Yet, stories like these are only the tip of the iceberg. Little do we realize that the "overnight" success stories actually start in the last hundred meters of the marathon where the underdog passes the favorite at the last moment. Rarely do we see the years of strenuous labor, sacrifice, opposition, failures, and small successes that finally lead to the breakthrough that attracts the media's attention. The backstory of all the work is not flashy. It doesn't sell. Overnight success is a racy fiction novel, a story taken out of context to paint a picture of a naturally gifted man or woman who overcame great odds to find him or herself in the Hall of Fame.

Success is the accumulation of small choices over time compounded with thousands of daily wins and tens of thousands of failures. Each small success is nothing in and of itself, but combined with the choice of learning from and overcoming failures, a reputation is built, character is established, a skill is cultivated, and little by little, success grows like a tree from a seed. This is another "slow and steady wins the race" principle, but the nuance to be noticed is that skill comes from commitment to the fundamentals.

The reverse is also true of the "unlucky." Instead of building daily upon a foundation of faithfulness, small steps, and right choices, the "unlucky" person cuts corners. Instead of focusing on how to build a legacy, the urgency to "arrive" causes them to take shortcuts, sacrificing quality and integrity for quick and cheap success. Weak foundations are laid. Facades are put up, and once the weight of success starts to come their way, the foundation cracks, and the pretense is exposed. Success will continue to move along to find a structure stable enough to hold its weight. Those in ruin will feel unlucky, when the truth is they did not put in the work that was required to sustain success.

One cannot throw up a lean-to, wave the flag of "cool new thing here," and expect to survive. No, we must bore laboriously into the rock. We must lay a solid foundation of faithfulness and consistency. We need to choose the right materials so that in the years to come, the building will stand as a landmark of success, of greatness, regardless of which flag may or may not be waving.

Being extreme, or "revolutionary", is not a sustainable or effective way to position yourself to seize the opportunity when it comes your way. You need to be noteworthy. You must stand out. You have no choice but to innovate and continue to grow with the world around you. To do this you do not need more excitement, a grander vision, more wildness, or crazier radicalness. You innovate and grow through the honing of your skill, which comes from practice, practicing when others quit because they became bored and a more exciting option popped up.

By all means, adopt the new thing, apply the innovation, be cutting edge, and have a great vision, but let the baseline of your operation be a commitment to your core values, even when everyone else is changing their values to win the masses.

You must commit to the rudimentary building block of your life and your trade. Becoming excellent in the basics will make you a master of what is highly sophisticated and complex. Zigzagging back and forth to attract attention will not progress your cause, grow your audience, or improve your life. Staying on a course in the face of the mundane, and the face of difficulties is what will set you apart in ten or twenty years.

Tools

1) Determine your Ark: Take a moment and honestly think about the dream that you want to chase. Don't pick the cool hot topic dream that all your friends are talking about. Ask yourself what YOU want to do and accomplish.

2) Find your 100-year pace: Noah fell trees and split trees for 100 years. What is the hard, unromantic work that you must commit to so that you might see your dream fulfilled in your lifetime?

3) Don't waver: When pressure comes to join the hottest bandwagon that distracts you from the true purpose of your life, and dream in your heart, remember DARE and "Just say no." Drugs aren't cool, and being blown too and fro by every fad isn't cool either.

CHAPTER TWO

Anchored is Shutting-up

Years ago, I stood in a conference with three hundred young people, dreaming about how awesome they are going to be. The speaker told everyone to write down their dream, get into small groups, share it with each other, and then encourage others to do their dream. Afterwards, the speaker opened the microphone for people who wanted to share their dream in a single sentence. When each dream was uttered, the crowd erupted in praise and encouragement.

I've thought back often on that moment and wondered how many of those people actually put their hand to the plow and saw that dream come to pass. How many more will look back on that moment fifty years from now with regret, saying, "I had a dream once, but . . . " Sadly, there are graveyards full of dreams and accomplishments the world was never able to see. We love talking about ambitions, but embarking down the lonely road and aligning our actions with our ambitions is entirely different.

King Solomon is considered to be the wisest man that ever lived. He accomplished more than many could ever hope or imagine. He built and ruled a kingdom and wrote many proverbs and sage-like reflections on wealth, success, and love. He had much to say about dreaming big and bringing those dreams to life. King Solomon once said, "Where there is no vision, the people perish."[4] If we don't have a vision for why we are living, a goal toward which we are striving, or a dream set before us, we lose motivation, discipline, and eventually, we die.

When dreams grow bigger and we start talking about how we are "gonna" do all these amazing thing—that is when you know you are getting blinded by your big talk and little action. When we start dreaming big, it's only natural to get excited. We start talking about our amazing dreams, telling our friends the great things we are destined to do. "I'm going to create this, do that, write this book—InSha'aAllah (Lord Willing), of course!" We tack on that last part as a formal qualifier, but to use later as a loophole to get us off the hook when we don't put in the work to write that book, pursue that other amazing dream, or start that business.

"Anything is possible," those around us say. As we listen to our friends' dreams, we begin to "dream bigger," too. Our dreams grow bigger, and our friends and leaders challenge us to dream bigger still. Soon, we find ourselves sitting around campfires, conference tables, and coffee shops telling each other how awesome we are. "Surely, *you* will be a billionaire. Wow."

At night, we go to bed smiling, feeling full and satisfied. "Yes, I really am going to change the world with my tech start-up" we whisper to ourselves, our bellies full of empty words, our egos sufficiently stroked.

The next morning though, it all becomes vanity as we forget to translate our words into action. As King Solomon wrote, "In all toil there is profit, but mere talk tends only to poverty."[5] Merely talking about our dreams and visions won't get us anywhere. Only doing the work and toiling over our dreams will net us a profit.

Don't get me wrong, there's nothing wrong with brainstorming with friends or championing one another. Voicing our dreams can also help us articulate what is in our hearts, connect us with like-minded friends who can partner with us, and help us sort out our hang-ups. If we deny ourselves the opportunity to share our dreams, goals, or visions, it can produce a burning dissatisfaction within us, driving us to achieve our ambitions. Talking about dreams, visions, and stirring up emotions might feel like movement, but talk alone will not accomplish anything.

If you find yourself talking constantly about your dreams, ask yourself why. Could it stem from insecurity, the hope that someone will come along and affirm the dream in your heart? Searching for approval is a slippery slope that will almost never turn out well.

When you share your dream, there are only four possible outcomes:

1. The person with whom you share your dream will think you and your idea are brilliant. The praise you receive can potentially produce a feeling of satisfaction as if you have already completed the task—weakening your motivation to actually step out and do it.

2. The person will find your idea stupid and assume you're an idiot, leaving you discouraged and tempted to discard the dream altogether.

3. The person will be neutral, leaving you insecure and wondering if your idea is good enough, causing you to postpone action until the dream is more clearly defined.

4. The person will offer help, resources, connections, accountability, encouragement, critical and refining feedback, or partnership to enable you start fulfilling your dream today.

If you or the people with whom you share your dream are not secure in their own identity and personhood, one or both of you could be left in one of the following positions:

1. You'll think you're better than the other person, creating a sense of false security and reducing your drive to pursue your dream.

2. You'll feel inferior to the other person, causing you to tweak your dreams to make them appear

more successful and/or work harder out of a spirit of comparison.

Either way, sharing your dream with the wrong person or for the wrong motives could sabotage your ambitions.

Some believe sharing your dreams, will cause you to accomplish them due to external peer pressure. Yet, this contrary to the findings of modern psychology. Studies shows that intrinsic motivation is a more powerful force than extrinsic motivation.

In 1985, Theresa Amabile, an associate professor of psychology at Brandeis University, asked seventy-two creative writers at Brandeis and at Boston University to write poetry. Some students were given a list of extrinsic (external) reasons for writing, such as impressing teachers, making money, and getting into graduate school, and were asked to think about their own writing with respect to these reasons. Others were given a list of intrinsic reasons: the enjoyment of playing with words, satisfaction from self-expression, and so forth. A third group was not given any list.

The results were clear. Students given the extrinsic reasons not only wrote less creatively than the others, as judged by twelve independent poets, but the quality of their work dropped significantly. Rewards, Amabile says, have this destructive effect primarily with creative tasks, including higher-level problem-solving. "The more complex the activity, the more it's hurt by extrinsic reward," she said. "Finally, extrinsic rewards can erode intrinsic interest. People who see themselves as working for money, approval or competitive success find their tasks less pleasurable, and therefore do not do them as well."[6] When we look to outside affirmation (extrinsic motivation) to encourage us to pursue a goal—our drive to achieve our goal erodes.

Loved ones, friends, and family who pat you on the back when you fail to follow through and tell you, "It's okay, you tried. You are amazing just as you are," can also hinder you. While these statements may be true, the fact remains that you failed to actualize your dream. You fell short of who you wanted to become.

Well-meaning friends who shower you with praise, saying, "Oh wow, your start-up company is going to be great!" are inadvertently feeding you sweet poison. Upon hearing such praise, it's easy to think, "You're right, it will be great . . . it *is* great. Whoa, I am great, I am accomplished." Without realizing it, you fall under an illusion, believing your dreams alone make us great. We start to believe that good intentions are more important than right action. Friends who say they believe in you but never challenge the integrity of your words are dangerous.

Yes, you need to speak life over your dreams. You must, however, be careful with who your share your dreams with. True friends will speak the truth, though painful, yet enemies will flatter you. Real friends challenge you to press on. Enemies coddle the soul and flesh when strength fails.

Flattery is a trap. A person who flatters their friends are setting them up for failure. When a friend flatters you, they are deceiving you. Yet, we are addicted to feedback, ideas, and encouragement, always feeling the urge to check with another friend, receive more praise, and become even less motivated to embark on our dream. What we are really seeking is acceptance, approval, and affirmation. We seek to justify, or qualify, ourselves before people rather than instruction for building a strong foundation for our dreams.

If you have friends who challenge you and hold you to the integrity of your word, you are blessed. You would do well by keeping those people close to you, as painful as it might be. Otherwise, people will either praise you with their tongue, killing your drive, or tell you that you can't do it, killing your dreams.

The solution? Keep your mouth shut. Work more than you talk. As the Arabic proverb goes, "The talk of the night amounts to nothing in the morning." Don't wake up on the other side of time with nothing but journals full of unfulfilled dreams. To see your dreams become more than a scribble in your notebook, you must work hard. You must venture from all that is familiar and comfortable, and most likely, you will need to go alone—at least at the beginning. Dreaming will not improve your life. Doing will.

Tools

Don't over share. Do You have a good idea? Awesome. Buy some duct tape, put it over your mouth, and get to work. Don't talk about it. As Nike says, "Just do it." Stop talking and start working.

Put your head down and produce something—then you can start talking.

Exercise: Write down one thing that you will accomplish this week. Don't tell anyone until you complete your task.

CHAPTER THREE

Anchored is Doing First

Do you talk but fail to start? You can always provide a world of excuses for not embarking on your dreams.

When my wife and I arrived to the Middle East, we felt completely overwhelmed, under-organized, unprepared, and ill equipped to start life in a foreign nation with little to no friends and a six-month-old baby. We could not count the number of days that started and ended in tears. We felt helpless, alone, misunderstood.

Our loving friends would call from back home and share about their amazing lives. They would relate how their business was exploding, and their relationships thriving. When they asked us how life was going, we could only relate to them how we were drowning in loneliness, confused by cultural faux pas, and exhausted from the culture shock and transition.

We didn't feel ready when we started our journey. It was only after two years of tireless work that we began to feel to be equipped to live and work abroad. Knowledge didn't equip us. Experience equipped us.

One cause for lack of action is we live in an environment over saturated with information, causing us to feel under-equipped. There is always one more Ted[x] Video to watch, one more start-up lecture to attend, and one more book to read (like this one). But reading more or attending another lecture won't get you closer to your goal. Doing the work with your hands is the one and only thing that will cause you to advance in any area of life.

There is a distinct difference between the Western and the Eastern mindsets. The Western mindset makes a clear distinction between the natural and the supernatural, thinks in a linear fashion, and calculates a person's worth based on money, material possessions, and power. The Western mindset also believes that competition is good and that history is an objective and chronological account of the facts.

The Eastern mindset makes no distinction between the natural and the supernatural. It thinks contextually and cyclically rather than linearly. Worth is derived from relationships with friends and family, and belonging is valued over achievement. The Eastern mindset believes history is an attempt to preserve significant truths in meaningful or memorable ways, whether or not the details are objectively true.[7]

Another key difference is the opposing cultural view on knowledge. The Western mindset operates out of the premise that "knowledge is power." Knowledge is good, and in the information age, knowledge is truly powerful. Too much knowledge, however, can lead us to overanalyze, which leads to indecision and paralysis.

The Eastern mind does not exalt knowledge to such a high position. Rather, it elevates action over understanding. In the East, "doing" has a higher value than "knowing." Negative attributes can spring from the eastern mindset by acting rashly without considering the implications.

The Eastern mindset believes outward actions lead to inward transformation, which results in greater understanding. This is not to say those operating under the Eastern mindset always act irrationally, but it does mean they are more willing to act on half-baked ideas. This pattern tends to frustrate Western thinkers, who can't understand why someone didn't have the foresight to build a bigger parking lot when expanding an airport from servicing 400,000 to 4,000,000 people a year.

In the West, it is common to hear the following sort of teaching:

> First, you must gain knowledge. In time, as you begin to fully understand why you should do something, you will gain a heart and passion for the project. As the knowledge and understanding trickles down from your head to your heart, it will start to transform you. As your heart is transformed, you will begin to live out of the passion in your heart, and your hands will there for act based on the values in your heart.

This is a great teaching and a fabulous analogy of how we work as individuals. I have used this logic before. The Eastern Mind, however, takes the opposite route.

While the West moves from head to heart to hands, the East moves from hands to heart to head. For example, according to the Eastern mind, to learn business, open a company and begin to sell products. As we sell we will intuitively become better sales people and be able to base our decision on gut feeling. Before long we will grow in knowledge of why a product works in a market—and why it may fail. In time, action developed into heart or gut reaction which will grow into head knowledge, allowing us to articulate a business theory.

This is counter-intuitive to the way we teach in the West. Aspiring business men and women cram into classrooms to listen to a talking head drone on. Students absorb the information, gaining an intellectual understanding of the issue, hoping to one day apply the knowledge to their life. Over time, however, the students' ideas of greatness change from doing the work to teaching how to do the work. This is a natural progression, seeing as the talking head has become the role model. The goal shifts from starting a business, for instance, to becoming the person who teaches others how to start a business. The progression is to be expected. The students see value in the teaching, not the doing. So, to be valued, they begin to teach. Years later, most students end up teaching about the business but do not practice what they teach.

Western training produces people who feel under-qualified, who feel the continual need for more training. It produces people who feel they need to know more before they can start off on the right foot. Eastern training puts people in work before they feel fully equipped, because they will never feel fully equipped. Starting, however, without well thought through plan has been the frustration and demise of many a project. The Eastern mindset breaks people out of paralysis and equips them through their hands rather than their minds.

This is how apprenticeships work. Instead of a student sitting under an instructor and learning by listening to his or her teachings, the student is plunged into the work with their hands, making mistakes, and learning experientially rather than intellectually.

We were designed to learn experientially rather than merely intellectually. But, if we neglect to think critically, study a problem, and develop a methodology to solve problems—we will be frustrated, just as a builder would unable to build a tower without any blueprints.

Both critical thinking and intellectual understand and action are needed. The thought systems of the East and the West are incomplete without each out.

The Perfect Pot

There once was an art professor who decided to run an experiment. He split his class in half, telling one half to only make one pot for the entire semester, and their grade would rest on the quality of that pot. To the second half, he said they would be graded on quantity of pots produced—the more pots produced, the better the grade.

At the end of the semester, the professor chose the best *quality* pot each student from the quantity group created and put them on display alongside the quality pot each student from the other group had made. The professor brought in an outside expert to judge the quality of the pots produced, but he didn't tell the judge how the pots had been made.

Surprisingly, the best pots came from the group who produced a large quantity of pots. Their practice made for perfection, not their thinking, analyzing, or planning.

In the same way, if you desire to grow in public speaking, tweaking your PowerPoint presentation until it's perfect won't grow your skill—at least not very much. But if you start seeking opportunities to share with people, you will become more aware of what works to engage people and what doesn't.

If you want to be a writer, then write every day. You might think you already found your voice and target audience, but if you keep producing, you might be surprised to find out what your friends actually want to read in comparison to what you think they might want or need. You might also be surprised to find out what you enjoy writing about.

Stop over planning and start doing. You can always make improvements along the way.

It is important to have a vision or a dream. It's a good idea to support that vision with a three, five, or ten-year plan. A brilliant plan, however, without action is worthless. Don't be afraid to start with a half-baked idea. We must venture out before we know where we are going or how we will get there.

We must begin when no one else is interested—and follow those who have pioneered a way before anyone else follows. The work must be started for the dream to come to pass. Start with your hands, and your heart and head won't be far behind.

Tools

Stop over analyzing your life or waiting until you "feel ready". Make a simple but well thought through plan of action—and then start working with your hands today.

- Don't have the perfect workout plan? Make a simple plan—start doing pushups and burpees, and develop your regiment as you develop your muscles.
- Feeling unqualified? Apply the action step on the latest book you read (like this one) before jumping to the next book.
- Feeling under educated or untrained to start your dream business? Write down the simplest smallest form of your business idea—and then sell your product or service in its simplest form to friends, family, and strangers.

CHAPTER FOUR

Anchored is Daily Marches

It was the summer of 1910. Virtually the entire world had been explored, and in the minds of many, only one frontier remained—the South Pole. Thousands of miles away from civilization, Antarctica remained one of the last places untouched by the modern world.

Robert Scott from England and Roald Amundsen from Norway led two separate expeditions, racing each other to reach the bottom of the world for land and country. Both men had very different styles of leadership.

Scott patterned his exploration on previous explorers. Scott launched his expedition from the same start point as previous explorers.

Amundsen started sixty miles closer to the pole, cutting their round-trip journey by 120 miles.

Scott wanted to reach the pole and gather scientific data by collecting rocks, performing experiments, and surveying the land.

Amundsen focused on only one goal—getting to the pole first.

Scott equipped his company with motorized sleds that broke down, ponies that had to be put down, and dogs that were sent back because they were ill-suited for the journey. The result was Scott's men having to *pull* their 200-pound sleds for over 1,000 miles.

Amundsen put his faith in proper sled dogs due to his experience in Norway, which freed his men from exerting needless effort.

Scott failed prepare for the unexpected. He simply trusted in the experience of previous explorers.

Amundsen planned for the worst. Not only that, he and his men worked tirelessly to make their sleds and equipment as practical, durable, lightweight, and user-friendly as possible, resulting in lighter loads, faster sleds, and quicker setup and teardown times for their camp.

One last major difference that set Scott and Amundsen apart was their daily schedule. Scott and his men travelled as much each day as the weather and their strength allowed. When the weather permitted it, some days they trekked for up to nine hours straight. During inclement weather, they didn't leave their tents at all.

Amundsen, on the other hand, decided they would travel one-quarter of a degree of latitude every day—which is fifteen nautical miles or around twenty miles a day. Hiking twenty miles a day across Antarctica is hard but realistic. Through blizzards or sunshine, they marched twenty miles each day, no more and no less. On average, they spent five to six hours on their feet each day and up to sixteen hours resting in their tents.

The tragic outcome was as follows: Scott and his men ran out of food and water and died twelve miles short of their supply cache. Scott's company marched as far as they could when they were feeling in the groove and things were going in their favor and then waited for better luck when the circumstances were unfavorable. Some days they would exhaust themselves by marching for extraordinary stretches, and the next they wouldn't move at all. Their inconsistency killed their confidence, and they had no clear expectation for when—or if—they might reach the pole.[8]

In contrast, Amundsen and company reached the South Pole and returned with food to spare. Amundsen chose a pace that challenged his men but which was still attainable no matter the weather. Each day, they knew they were getting closer to their goal. Their consistency built their morale and gave them strength for the journey.

What can we learn from this story? For starters, circumstances change constantly. Some days the sun shines on us and we feel like we can do no wrong. On other days, the storms billow against us, nothing goes right, and we feel as if merely getting out of bed is success enough. If our work is dependent on our circumstance and mood, we will not travel far, and we may perish along the way. However, if we commit to executing a manageable amount of work each day, rain or shine, we shall overcome.

Professionals also show up when they don't feel like it and meet deadlines. Amateurs show up when they feel like it and don't have deadlines to meet. Though you may be an amateur in the eyes of the world, if you approach your craft like a professional, clocking in daily, rain or shine, eventually you will become a master.

Limiting Work

Long-term success is found by getting up and working hard on a daily basis, Yes. But there is more to it than "hard work". In the story of Scott and Amundsen's race to the South Pole, we see that Amundsen success was tied to marching every day, even when the men didn't feel like it, but they also implemented a second element. Amundsen limited the amount of work that his men could do on a given day.

Amundsen had *one* goal: get to the pole and back alive. Beyond that, he made sure that when his men were not hiking, they were resting. Amundsen also limited the number of miles they hiked each day. Even if the weather was perfect and the wind was at their back, allowing them to hike the distance in half the normal time, they still stopped at twenty miles. It was the limiting of the workload that enabled his men to do more over the long run.

Like Amundsen, you must place limits on productivity so that you might be productive. You can easily be fooled into believing that, "If a little is good, more is better." Water is good, but drinking too much water in a given time period will kill you. Limiting production can actually produce a higher, more sustainable, and better quality of work over decades.

Limiting the number of hours you work in a given day or week can be as important as making sure we show up and work hard. In human's I-am-above-average-thinking, people like to pretend they are exceptions to the rule, tricking themselves into believing a couple of extra hours of work will produce above-average results. This may be true for about a week before your humanity catches up with you.

Soon, your productivity will drop below average without you being aware of it. You will believe you are still doing an above-average job, but the facts will prove otherwise. What is most unfortunate is that when you do return to working normal hours, it will take a few weeks for your mind and body to recover before you are functioning at your peak level.[9]

We like to think that we can power through, but it is not a sustainable practice for a productive life. It merely places stress on our relationships, health, and our spirits. As faithful, diligent stewards of our souls, health, and families, we must limit the amount of time we spend working.

How much should you limit your workload? That is something you will have to explore for yourself. For assembly lines and industrial labor, that standard is forty hours a week. For people dealing with information, such as writers, musicians, programmers, bloggers, and so on, after thirty-five hours a week, the mind begins to weaken.[10] People working with creativity and information need time and extra sleep to allow creativity to grow and solutions to form. Much of our creative thinking and solutions comes from our subconscious mind. When learning a language, sleeping is the best tool available, because during sleep the mind transfers information from short-term to long-term memory and works hard to process sounds, grammar, and vocabulary. When stuck on a problem or suffering from a creativity block, sleep—even a short nap—will often produce answers and breakthroughs as well as increase performance and alertness.[11]

To discover how to function optimally, you need to measure your mental acuteness, your quality of work, and quantity of work over time.

Sleep Your Way to Productivity

In my early twenties, I looked at leaders around me who, so I thought, only needed four to six hours of sleep per night. I envied them, so I decided to give it a try. After a week of getting only six hours of sleep a night, I wound up sick, and it took a week or two before I returned to my normal level of productivity. But that was only the beginning of my experimentations with sleep.

In university, I found myself pulling one all-nighter a week as I struggled to finish reading books and writing papers. Because of this, I tried to switch to a forty-eight-hour day. I would stay up for thirty-six hours, working on papers through the night when no one could bother me, and then crash for twelve hours. That lasted for about a week before by body rebelled.

Then I tried going to bed at seven or eight in the evening so I could wake up at three or four in the morning and maximize my work time without distractions. That only lasted a week or two before life caught up to me once again.

As a result of my failures, I resented myself, and my body, for needing up to nine hours of sleep to feel rested and to function properly. I fought my "weakness" with all my strength. I dreamed of how amazing it would be to need only six hours of sleep. I fantasized about how much more I could accomplish if only my body would cooperate. I was an ignorant fool.

Sleeping eight hours a night and refusing to work overtime might be the most important thing you can do to increase your productivity. Getting less than eight hours of sleep can actually shorten your life and cause your productivity to decline sharply. In 2003, researchers from Harvard Medical School did a study on the effect of sleep deprivation. [12] They created three groups and had them sleep four, six, and eight hours a night for two weeks. They also had one group who received no sleep over a period of three days. All of the participants were held under standardized conditions over the course of the two weeks for those on the restricted sleep schedule and for the duration of the three days for those getting no sleep.

After two weeks, those getting eight hours of sleep each night showed no change in performance. Those who received four to six hours of sleep each night demonstrated decreasing performance levels and increasing sleepiness. The study found that the effects of sleep deprivation are cumulative. The longer the subjects were kept in a restrictive sleep environment, the worse their performance became. Even though the performance of the sleep-deprived participants continued to drop, the participants were not aware of it or their increased sleepiness.

The most shocking discovery of the study was that at the end of the two weeks, those who received six or less hours of sleep each night were functioning with the same motor skill, cognitive abilities, and decision-making abilities as participants who had not slept for forty-eight hours straight. The difference between those who didn't sleep for two days and those who were on a reduced sleep schedule over two weeks is that the latter group was dangerously unaware of their complete impairment.

What can we learn from this? The fastest way to improve your productivity is to stop working when you should be sleeping.

Sleep impacts not only your mental state but also your health. While you are sleeping, your body is working hard to clean up cell waste in the brain and repair the body. If you lack sleep, your body will not be able to perform these vital functions. Accumulative sleep deprivation can lead to high blood pressure and even death.[13,14]

If you are cutting into your sleep time in an effort to boost your productivity, you are deceiving yourself. Sleep well, and you will live and work well.

Schedule It, And It Will Happen

Studies from leading psychologists have shown that when an individual intends to achieve a task or change a habit, he or she is far more likely to follow through if the person sets a time in which he or she hopes to fulfill this goal or action. To put it simply, if you schedule it, it will happen.

In one study[15], researchers looked at the intention and implementation of people's desire to exercise. The study had three groups. One group was shown a motivational video and told to record how often they exercised over the next month. The second group did not receive a video and was told to report how often they exercised. The third group received a video and was told to schedule a time and place where they would exercise. The results were staggering. Only thirty-eight percent of the first group exercised regularly, and only thirty-five percent of the second group, but ninety-one percent of the third group exercised on a regular basis. The difference was not the motivational video but the scheduling of the activity. This goes to show that if you schedule time for your goals, you will achieve them at a higher rate than if you do not schedule them.

Most people don't have a problem wasting fifteen minutes of their day, but they would be terrified to squander their destiny. People who have no problem wasting fifteen minutes lack the understanding that their time is their destiny. If you squander your time, you will squander your destiny.

If you don't schedule your time someone or something else will schedule your time for you. Your life will be controlled by the "tyranny of the urgent." When you leave the hours of your day undecided, a relatively unimportant email can distract you from the important work that will further your vision and goals in life.

Scheduling your intentions is the hinge point of accomplishment. We can have endless metrics and get really excited staying up late reading on how we need more sleep, come up with complex formulas on improving different areas of our life by marginal percentages, and dream about how great our lives will be in ten years, but if we neglect the work of creating time to achieve our small action plans, we will remain nothing but dreamers.

Tools

Applying the lesson of the Twenty-Mile March is simple: take small, tangible steps towards a bigger goal. Decide where you want to go and then create an action plan that will take you there.

1) Write down *one*, only one, goal that you want to accomplish in the next 6 months.

2) What *small* step can you take each day so that in 6 month's you will have achieved your goal. (Ideally, the daily task can be completed in one or two hours.)

3) The task should be doing, learning, and growing from *experience*. For example, if you want to become better at photography, take and edit a few photos during the hour. If you want to grow in a particular relationship, write a letter, make a phone call, or grab a coffee with that person. Don't merely develop strategies. Develop action.

Don't be overwhelmed if you aren't sure what area to pick or how to progress. Start somewhere, head out, and in a week or months' time, you will not have lost anything even if you decide to change course. You will be on the road, and that is what matters.

CHAPTER FIVE

Anchored is Doing Less

Vilfredo Pareto was a leading economist, sociologist, and engineer in the 1800s. He is best known for the Pareto Principle, which is now known as the 80/20 Rule.[16] In short, the Pareto Principle explains the unequal distribution of wealth, income, land ownership, and production. Pareto stumbled upon this principle by observing how eighty percent of the land in France was owned by twenty percent of the population[17] and that eighty percent of his peas were produced by twenty percent of his pea plants.

Prior to discovering this principle, Pareto realized that if he wanted to increase his pea production by fifty percent, he would have to either a) designate more land to grow his peas, or b) try and squeeze fifty percent more plants into his pea patch. Both solutions presented glaring problems. The first option would cut into the rest of his garden, lowering his production of other important vegetables, or he might be limited on land. Increasing the plot size would also increase his workload. The second option would overcrowd the plot, degrade the soil, and ultimately cause all of his peas to suffer— most likely resulting in an overall decrease in production, permanent damage to his land, and an increased workload. Once armed with the discovery that eighty percent of his peas came from twenty percent of his plants, he was able to double his pea production while cutting his workload by nearly seventy percent.

Pareto and other economists over the past century have tested this principle and have found the 80/20 Rule holds true for many cases besides agriculture, although in some instances the spread is actually closer to 90/10 or 95/5.

We can apply this simple principle to our life, increasing our impact while decreasing our output and overall workload. Sometimes while trying to improve, grow, or mature we add activities, disciplines, or routines to our schedule with varying degrees of success. Building is human nature. However, even though it's easy to add activities, we can't add more hours to our days, so it doesn't take long to hit a glass ceiling. By applying the 80/20 Rule, we can examine our situation in new light.

To understand this, assume you have ten date palms. Two of the palms produce a total of 400 Kg of dates while the other eight palms only produce 80 Kg dates. If you rip up the eight palms that aren't producing, you will have cut your workload by eighty percent, freeing up your soil by eighty percent, and will have only lost twenty percent of your date production. If you were to find a date palm with traits similar to the high-producing palms, you would effectively increase your total production by twenty percent while cutting costs and your workload by seventy percent, giving you seventy percent more room in your garden for other kinds of plant. No longer do you have an issue with limited space, time, or resources.

Like Pareto, we all have a limited amount of real estate (time), and we all have a limited amount of resources within that real estate (focus and energy) from which we can draw. Like Pareto, we can observe where our results are coming from, and we can easily learn where we are wasting resources. For example, multitasking during dinner with family to get some extra things done for work will end up damaging our relationships and, in the long run, hurt our performance at work. Clearing less productive areas in our garden and planting a fraction of productive activities can give us more time and better results while exerting less energy.

As Pareto unearthed his discovery while gardening, gardeners have been exercising this principle for hundreds of generations under a different term: pruning.

We need to be productive, not merely busy. Like fruit trees, or rose bushes, we need to cut off the bushy branches that are sucking energy away from productive and meaningful areas of life. Just because there is a branch on a tree (fancy looking area of your life) doesn't mean the branch is productive. Yes, it may be a strong, good-looking branch, but if it isn't getting results, the branch isn't functioning as intended. A good gardener cuts the unproductive branches off so the plant will not waste energy, allowing the plant to put its limited resources into fruit-bearing branches only.

We were created to become great and successful. God, the ultimate gardener of our lives, is so committed to us that he cuts and prunes us carefully so we can grow into our most productive self. This is good, and potentially painful, news. We do not need to do *everything* or to be profitable in any and every way possible. We must be concerned with bearing the *maximum* amount of profit with the least amount of energy.

We all have unproductive branches in our lives that waste time, energy, and effort. Often, we feel obligated to keep feeding those branches. Maybe in a prior season the branch bore fruit, and lots of it. Yet now, for whatever reason, it is unfruitful. It is an obligation in our schedule that keeps demanding resources but never provides anything return. It can be quite difficult to prune such branches. There are often relational ties, invested resources (time, energy, money, emotions), unfulfilled hopes, or nostalgia connected with such branches. Maybe the branch is a project you started years ago but now you are merely maintaining it because ending it would feel like a failure, when it was only intended for a specific purpose for a short season. At times, it is harder to shut down a project than begin one. You may have taken time to fertilize and prune a certain project— but if its season is past, do not hesitate to hack it off.

When a good gardener sees a branch that has an enormous amount of fruit—the garden will prune, or trim, the branch so it will bear even greater profits. This optimizing of a system can be hard to do as it may seem like you are cutting off a successful project—and you are. But as you focus and streamline your life and activities you will see multiple times the returns in the areas that truly matter to you. At times, we are afraid to cut good things that seem good in our lives, because we can see their value. Yet, we don't realize that these areas are actually working against the greatest results our life is capable of producing.

The quantity of time you spend being busy does not equal fruitfulness or productivity. Running "urgent" errands, sitting through irrelevant meetings, or replying to emails can keep you quite busy while keeping you far away from the work that matters. Time spent does not always equate to time spent productively.

I used to believe that if I were busy continually I would end up being productive and successful.

To be more productive, you can't merely add more to your schedule, you must weed things out. If an area is unfruitful or unimportant, weed it out of your life so the fruit-bearing parts can flourish.

Tools

Here is a list of question to ask yourself to help determine what is fruit, and what is busyness that is stealing your time:

Where is the profit?

- What is "success"?
- Is there another way to define success that I may find more fulfilling?
- What activity is the greatest driver of my success?

Where is the waste?

- What activity makes my look good, but fails to drive results that attribute to success (i.e., endlessly analyzing stats, lengthy meetings)?
- What am I doing out of obligation that bears no lasting impact?
- What am I doing to impress or please people?
- What product, service, or relationship am I keeping alive that should have died long ago?
- What function do I perform that someone else could do quicker and better?

CHAPTER SIX

Anchored is Improving One-Percent

Life is a marathon. We can agree that slow and steady wins the race. We know that showing up each day and putting in our reps is what will cause us to be successful years from now. No matter what you're trying to accomplish or what area you develop—fitness or health, songwriting, gardening, relationships, language learning, cooking—it is a marathon that you will need to sustain for the rest of your life. Taking the small, seemingly insignificant steps each day is what will lead to proficiency and maturity in life. Faithfulness—not talent, skill, or sheer "awesomeness"—is the mark of greatness. But what can set us apart from every other person who is putting in his or her minimum required reps?

Jerry Rice, one of the greatest quarterbacks ever to play America Football, said, "Today I will do what others won't, so tomorrow I can accomplish what others can't." Every player in the American Football League (the NFL) is at the top of his game. Every NFL player is working out, eating healthy, training consistently. What set Rice apart from every other player was that he pushed himself to do one more rep and to get on the field fifteen minutes earlier than the other players.

In team workouts he was famous for his hustle. While many receivers would trot back to the quarterback after catching a pass, Rice would sprint to the end zone after each reception. Typically, he would continue practicing long after the rest of the team had gone home.

Most remarkable were his six-days-a-week off-season workouts, which he conducted entirely on his own. While the rest of the NFL players were taking the summers slow, Rice worked out *harder* than he would normally do during the regular season. Mornings were devoted to cardiovascular work, running a hilly five-mile trail. He would reportedly run ten forty-meter wind sprints up the steepest part. In the afternoons he did equally strenuous weight training. These workouts became legendary as the most demanding in the league, and other players joined Rice sometimes to see what it was like. Some of them got sick before the day was over.

Rice was also known for changing his routine as not to fall into a comfortable habit. He challenged his body constantly to perform in different ways, not merely improving his forty-meter dash.

Similarly, in learning and education, growth only occurs when the mind is being challenged consistently at a level that is one or two steps above its current capabilities. In language learning, new words must always be added for old words to be solidified into the long-term memory. To grow vocabulary, a reader must read material that contains around ten to twenty percent unknown vocabulary, grammar, and expressions. Those who excel at language learning are challenging their abilities even when they don't need to be. They place themselves in awkward and uncomfortable situations on purpose so there is a greater demand placed upon their language, forcing them to expend more energy than normal and, thereby, expanding their capacity.

Anders Ericsson, a psychologist at Florida State University who is best known for his work concerning the 10,000 Hour Rule[18], explains that, "You don't get benefits from mechanical repetition, but by adjusting your execution over and over to get closer to your goal. You have to tweak the system by pushing, allowing for more errors at first as you increase your limits." We grow by pushing our boundaries constantly to be outside of our grasp.

If we only apply the 80/20 rule, the 20-mile march, or optimizing our sleep schedule without pushing ourselves to take steps that no one around us cares to do, we will end up mediocre. We will be less than extraordinary. We must challenge ourselves in the areas where we have become comfortable in our habits, routines, and performance—pushing ourselves to take one more step that we didn't think we were capable of achieving.

Ask yourself these questions:

1) What are others around you *unwilling* to do today which could set them apart tomorrow?
2) What is it you would like to do tomorrow that others are *unable* to do?
3) What can you do *today* to ensure you can perform your dream *tomorrow*?

One Percent

In all the years of the Tour-de-France, France had never won their nation's own competition. That is, not until 2010, when the French cycling team hired a man named Dave Brailsford to coach them.

With the daunting task of winning the Tour-de-France before him, you might think Brailsford needed to be radical and change everything, like in the movies. Cue the *Rocky* soundtrack over a montage of Brailsford yelling and encouraging his team to train harder, to give it 110 percent. I can imagine them working out in the pouring rain, on the verge of giving up, when by some supernatural force, they find one last ounce of energy to push through to the end. Wow! The team has never trained so hard. Race day comes, and Dave gives the classic even-if-you-lose-I-will-be-proud-of-you-and-you-should-be-proud-of-yourselves-for-you-know-you-gave-it-all pep talk. Dave is proud, and he has never seen a group of men work so hard towards a common goal.

Wrong. Insert screeching soundtrack and tangling film here.

Instead, he suggested that they look at every component of bike racing and try to improve it by one percent. That's it, a boring one percent.

Dave tore apart what it means to race. He looked at everything: tires, bike engineering, race suits, seats, diet, hygiene, pillows, mattresses, and more.[19] He and his team examined each area to see how they could improve it by one percent.

He taught his racers to wash their hands properly so that they would get sick less often. He also optimized their diets. Would two fewer colds a year win the race? No, but it would improve their overall health and the consistency of their training. They studied sleep patterns. They researched pillows and mattresses that would optimize their sleep, bringing them to each hotel along the twenty-one-day trek. Would getting a better night sleep cause them to win? No, but it would allow them to be slightly more rested than the rest of the field. They revised how they did team meetings. They created a new format, reducing the amount of time spent in boardrooms. Would changing how the team held their meetings have a large impact on winning a bike race? No, but it might increase their communication and productivity.

Dave's plan worked—but not as he thought. Dave hoped this plan would be able to win the Tour-de-France in five years. He was wrong. It took three years, not five.

There are many reasons why Brailsford's idea of "marginal gains," as his approach is now called, had a rapid and noticeable impact on their team. First, when competing at such a high level of excellence, there is very little difference between teams. Those racing at this level are already in the top 0.0001 percent of their field. The level of skill and athleticism between the world champion and the person who finished in the middle of the pack is negligible. Likewise, in golf, there is only a 1.4 stroke difference between a world champ and the rest of the field. Second, the combined sum of improving ten or twelve components by a negligible amount creates a noticeable difference on the whole. Third, these small gains over time act like compounding interest. When you improve an area by one percent, the impact over a short period of time is negligible, but in a year's time you will be a completely different person. The converse is also true. If you make a compromise that decreases efficiency by one percent, the depreciation will not be felt within a few days, but in a few years, you will be an exponentially different person, but for the worse.

Tools

There are seven core spheres of life:
1. Spirituality (prayer, fasting, worship)
2. Relationships (family, friends, co-workers.)
3. Vocation (vocation, career, education)
4. Charity (volunteering, helping others)

5. Economics (spending, giving, saving, investing)
6. Physicality (exercise, health, diet)
7. Rest (recreation, vacation, play, entertainment, sports)

Identify short, and long-term goals for each of these seven areas of your life. Break down each of these seven areas of your life into smaller components—the smaller the better. As you break down these areas identify small changes you can easily tweak 1% creating compounding gains over time.

As you uncover areas needing improvement, work to discover the root of the issue. If you are able to tweak the root you will be able to see a cascading affect with little effort.

One simple tool is to ask "why?" until you've narrowed into the root cause of your problem. Fix the root, don't waste energy on micromanaging your bad fruit. For example:

Problem: You are not trusted with leadership responsibilities and it is hurting your career.
Why: You are consistently late.
Why: You fail to leave your house on time.
Why: You consistently wake up late
Why: You stay up too late.
Why: Because you are staring at your phone or TV too late causing you to not be able to fall asleep

Solution: Consider putting down your phone or turning off the TV at least hour before you need to go to sleep so that you are getting at least 8 hours of rest.

By identifying and fixing root issues we are able to leverage our time and energy resulting into disproportionate returns over time.

CHAPTER SEVEN

Anchored is Taking Responsibility

It was March 13, 1964, at 2:30 am, Kitty Genovese a 28-year-old bar tender finished her shift at Ev's Eleventh Hour Bar, jumped into her red Fiat, and drove home.

Winston Mosely, married with three kids, sat in his parked car off Hoover Ave looking to "kill a woman,"[20] saw Kitty stop at the traffic light ", and decided to follow her home.

When Kitty arrived at her apartment at 3:15am. As she walked to her apartment door, Winston jumped out of his car with a hunting knife.

Kitty ran for the door. But Winston grabbed her stabbing her twice in the back.

Kitty screamed, "Oh my God, he stabbed me! Help me!"

A neighbor heard the scream and shouted out the window, "Let that girl alone!" That was enough to scare Winston off who jumped in his car and drove away.

For ten minutes Kitty laid screaming on the ground, nearly unconscious and locked out of the apartment. No one helped her.

After ten minutes, Winston changed his mind and returned to the scene of the crime. He attacked her again. He raped her. He stabbed her 12 more times before fleeing the scene the with $49-dollar Kitty had in her pursue. All while 38 witnesses watched from their apartment windows.

An ambulance arrived at 4:15 AM, an hour after the attack began. Kitty died on the way to the hospital. According to one report of the story,

> "The attack had lasted 35 minutes. During police investigations, it was found that 38 people in the surrounding apartments had witnessed the attack, but only one had eventually called the police. One couple (who said they assumed someone else had called the police) had moved two chairs next to their window in order to watch the violence."[21]

Most of these individuals assumed someone else had called the police or did not want to get involved. They had a sense it was not their responsibility. Someone else would call the Police. Someone else would help. One witness even confessed that they, "Did want to get involved," another admitted he "turned up the radio so he wouldn't hear the woman's screams."[22] After all it wasn't their responsibility.

Why, with so many people witnessing this horrific crime, didn't more than one person call the police? Why didn't someone come to her aid?

After many studies, articles, and findings we now understand the phenomenon we know today as the "Diffusion of Responsibility."[23] Diffusion of Responsibility is,

> "a sociopsychological phenomenon whereby a person is less likely to take responsibility for action or inaction when others are present. Considered a form of attribution, the individual assumes that others either are responsible for taking action or have already done so." [24]

Diffusion of responsibility happens because individual group members believe they are not responsible to act, that someone else has acted already, or that somebody will act in the future.[25]

The immediate application of this story is to remember that when you are in a group—it is your responsibility to stand up and do something. Don't assume someone else is going to act. But, there is a broader application to apply to our dreams, goals, work, and everyday life, not merely emergency situations.

When we are in a group (and we always exist within a group in some form or another—even when you are alone), it is easy to hide and assume someone else will come along and act upon our behalf.

If we stick within the confines of the group, if we fall in line with all the thought processes, actions, and inaction of the group—we will cease to take personal action upon our goals. Our level of personal responsibility and initiative will decrease. We must set out by ourselves. We must go alone—and take action that no one else in the group is currently taking.

When we set out by ourselves, we cannot abdicate responsibility for our lack of initiative or diligence. It all falls on us. Groups have their place, but they can also give us license to slack off, because we know others around us will make up for our lack of initiative.

Many people are sitting on the fence, waiting for someone to grab their arm and say, "Hey, that's my dream, too. Let's find others and go together." Unfortunately, this scenario is unlikely to happen. Only by stepping out alone, and taking personal responsibility for our own life, do we find companions for the journey.

No one can chase your dreams for you. No one is able to be more passionate about your dreams than you. We must be internally motivated to chase our dreams. Starting alone is one of the best ways to forge that internal motivation.

When we start pursing a dream alone in our closet, where no one sees and no one knows—whether it be launching a business, becoming a photojournalist, or beginning to exercise—the nursery of our labor is not sustained by the praise of people or comparison. Rather, the achievement is our own, and our failure is not a public shame. Laboring in the closet is like walking around knowing a secret that no one else knows besides God. All the naysayers won't have the chance to say nay, and all the flatterers won't have the opportunity to praise. Accomplishing your goal will become a landmark between you and God. When your first marathon is over, album is completed, book published, painting sold, or coffee served, you will smile when your friend remarks, "Wow I didn't know that you could do that." Inside, you'll think, "That's because I didn't do it for you."

It's easy to believe having a group of like-minded people around you will pave your path with support, encouraging you to step out and pursue your dream. While this might be true, it is not always the case. In groups, or community, we often wait for a leader to stand up and act. We fear our ideas aren't good enough. We fear we aren't qualified. We hide within the group waiting for someone else to lead, preserving our reputation and steering clear of opposition and rejection.

Setting out alone is scary, but before long, you will become connected with others who have gone before you—and those who follow your example.

Tools

It is your responsibility to the world around you to stand up and take responsibility.

- What have you wanted to do but haven't started because others aren't on board?
- How can you set out alone without the help of others?
- Are you constantly asking, Why the government, or society, or your superiors aren't doing something about a particular issue or apparent need? This is an indicator you should stand up and take responsibility and being to act to bring a solution to this problem you are passionate about.

CHAPTER EIGHT

Anchored is Influencing

Derek Sivers, the founder of CD Baby, gave a TED talk about how to start a movement. The focus of his talk was a video of a shirtless dancing man in the middle of a crowd at an outdoor music festival. The film starts with the man dancing in a ridiculous manner. People look at him as if he is a crazed, lone nut—which he *is*. Moments later though, a second man enters the frame and begins dancing. The first man acknowledges him, gives him some goofy dance pointers, and then they rock out together. The second dancing man, whom Sivers calls the "First Follower," calls someone to join him. He leaves the screen for a moment and then returns with several others. Momentum builds. Those who were on the fence now feel it is safe to join in. No longer is it a lone nut—it is now a movement. Within thirty seconds, the tables have turned completely. People rush to join the fray, more afraid of being the odd one out than dancing like a fool.

Very few of us are like the shirtless dancing man or even the First Follower, willing to step out of the crowd and make a splash. Only after things have reached a tipping point do most of us join in. As we learned with Kitty Genovese, however, relying on the crowd to carry you to where you want to go is foolishness. Even if you see only one other person doing what you want to be doing, join him or her. You may not get the credit, but you will know you were responsible for catalyzing a movement.

If we take what we learned in the previous chapter on taking responsibility and stepping out and apply it to the story of the shirtless dancer and first follower we learn two lessons.

First—If no one else is dancing. If no one else is "living your dream"—the become the crazy-shirtless-dancer-guy. Take responsibility for your life. Step out of the crowd. But we do not step out of the crowd to be rebellious, we step out to start a movement. We step out to model and encourage others to break free of the status quo and do something great, something different, something right, something better. The entire purpose of taking a bold step by yourself is so that others can follow in the path you have forge. We step out of the crowd, to bring the crown with us.

But how? How do we spark an idea? How do we move people into action?

The shirtless dancer was a lone nut. Everyone was laughing at him . . . until something happened. He was a lone nut, until he got his first follower.

The first follower was the big turning point. Someone came along and said, "Yes! I want to dance and have a great time too." The nut could have shunned his follower and said, "I'm dancing, this is my space, stop stealing my spot light." But instead he accepted his first followed and helped, him he taught him how to dance like we was.

After this the real magic happens—the first follower, after being accepted and empowered by the lone nut, went out and invited a few friends to come join, "Don't be on the outside of this party! Join in!" The first follower went out and empowered other to dance like a goof too.

If you are a lone nut—you need to find and embrace your first follower. Pour into the one or two people around you—don't focus on getting the crowds to join in with you. Put your energy into the ones and two around you and watch your idea multiply.

This reminds me of a famous word problem. You've probably heard it, too: Would you rather have $1 million today or a penny today, two pennies tomorrow, four pennies the next day, and so on for a month (31 days)? Anyone who hasn't seen the problem before would likely choose the $1 million, because how far could a few pennies go? However, if you look at the chart to the right, you might change your mind.

Days	Amount given each day	Accumulative sum
1	$0.01	$0.01
2	$0.02	$0.03
3	$0.04	$0.07
4	$0.08	$0.15
5	$0.16	$0.31
6	$0.32	$0.63
7	$0.64	$1.27
8	$1.28	$2.55
9	$2.56	$5.11
10	$5.12	$10.23
11	$10.24	$20.47
12	$20.48	$40.95
13	$40.96	$81.91
14	$81.92	$163.83
15	$163.84	$327.67
16	$327.68	$655.35
17	$655.36	$1,310.71
18	$1,310.72	$2,621.43
19	$2,621.44	$5,242.87
20	$5,242.88	$10,485.75
21	$10,485.76	$20,971.51
22	$20,971.52	$41,943.03
23	$41,943.04	$83,886.07
24	$83,886.08	$167,772.15
25	$167,772.16	$335,544.31
26	$335,544.32	$671,088.63
27	$671,088.64	$1,342,177.27
28	$1,342,177.28	$2,684,354.55
29	$2,684,354.56	$5,368,709.11
30	$5,368,709.12	$10,737,418.23
31	**$10,737,418.24**	**$21,474,836.47**

As you can see, the numbers grow slowly, gaining momentum, until they achieve astronomical amounts seemingly overnight. The sum gains 96.875% of the total amount in only the last five days. If we change the time period from days to years, we can see how people might think success happens over a course of five years.

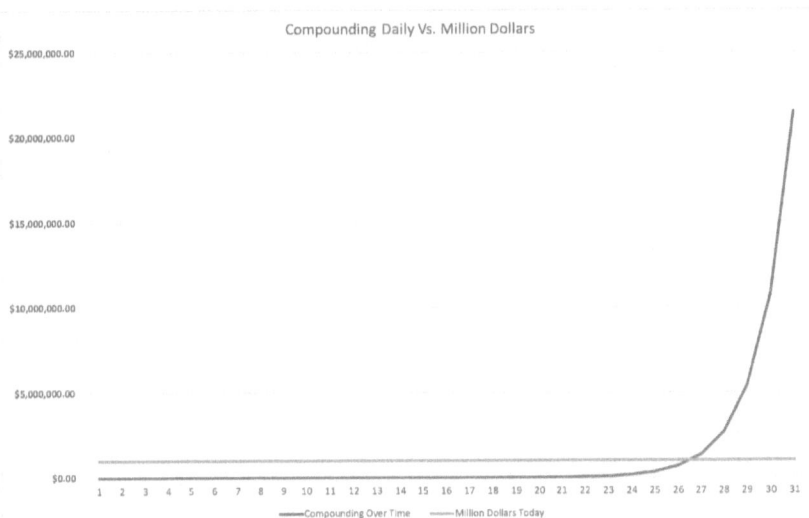

Yet, the chart shows otherwise—it was twenty-six hard years of little wins leading up to five years of massive success.

Platforms and Influence

In a world where everyone is building their personal platforms, brands, and become social media influencer, many are dreaming of getting a lucky break, getting on TV, speaking to packed out stadiums, holding blowout concerts, record book sales, and millions of followers on Instagram, LinkedIn, and YouTube.

Many people do in fact fill stadiums, build multi-million-dollar businesses, and touch billions through their lives and work. Those who hold massive influence play an important role in human history. Yet, these people did not start in stadiums, they started on street corners, ghettos, garages, pubs, and dives with the poor, insignificant, and forgettable people. Yet, through their diligence they have been exalted and entrusted with much.[26]

If, instead of filling a stadium, you connected in a meaningful way with the same two people every week for a year, teaching a skill, selling them on your product, and then instructed them to sit down with two people every week for a year, teaching everything you had taught them, your voice would spread around the globe with incredible speed and efficiency. This is the basic idea of multi-level marketing and basic idea of coaching and mentorship. This process has powerful compounding effects.

Within thirteen years, one million people would have been mentored for fifty-two hours each and would themselves begin to help others as you are doing. Many would surpass you in skill and understanding. After 21 years, over 6.9 billion people would have been touched though your small amount of work. This is quite the success story. Yet, you personally would have only come into contact with forty-two people over the course of those twenty-one years.

Maybe you are a skeptic. Maybe you think, "Well not all those people you talk to will follow through and talk to others, at least half will fail to follow through." Fair enough. If half the people dropped off in the process, it would take around thirty-three years to reach the globe.

The math is simple; the numbers clear. If you stay small, if you focus on making a deep change in a single individual, you will leave an impact far more significant and widespread than if you only worked to reach millions of people through wide but shallow marketing ploys.

Put your energy into small things with deep impact. Start by putting your energy into the individuals right in front of you. If you do this and teach others to do the same, you will achieve your goals within your lifetime—even though only forty people might remember your name.

Simple people like you and me can have a profound impact on the world through one-on-one engagement and relationship. We don't need someone to pick us. We don't need to wait until our platform or audience is big enough. Start now.

Therefore, go—plant the seeds of life and truth in the hearts of those around you. Become the greatest influencer the world has seen through pouring your life's energy into the ones and twos around you.

Break free of analysis that leads to paralysis… the constant "learning" that disempowers our ability to create. Instead, step outside the bounds of the status quo, to leave comfort and safety behind, and set out alone. Knowing *exactly* where we are going isn't imperative. The important factor is that we are setting out and *doing* the dream written on our heart, and not waiting for the dream to be done for us. Sometimes that requires us to take uncomfortable steps forward when no one else is on board (like the shirtless dancer). Other times, it means following someone or something that we believe in when no one else is following (like the first follower)—thereby starting a movement. Note, it was the first person who followed the lone nut that started the movement. Both are important, and both are valuable. Do not shrink back from being the lone nut, or the first follower.

Tools

If you want to reach the masses you must first learn to impact a single person in a genuine way.

1) Identify one person or client that you feel drawn to mentor or coach. Pour your time, energy, and even money into them, and then teach them to do the same with others.

   a. It doesn't have to be super formal. You aren't becoming their Yoda. Basically, help them reach their goals—and empower them to help others reach their goals.

2) Pay attention: Take note of what impacts their life in a deep way and take note of what remains as surface fluff.

3) Rinse and repeat.

CHAPTER NINE

Anchored is Finishing

An anchored life is one of following through on your commitments—no matter how hard it hurts, and finishing what you started. All successful people possess this quality—they keep their commitments, that is they keep their word, and they finish what they start. Doing these two simple actions will make you a trustworthy person, and a reliable person.

It doesn't matter if you want to be a successful mom, successful athlete, or a successful business leader—you must keep your word for people to trust you. If people cannot trust that you will follow through with your commitments, over time, they will pull back from their commitment to the relationship. Finishing what we start is imperative to reaching our goals and achieving the success we are searching for. This would seem like a no brainer—and yet many in this generation are breaking their word, commitment, and leave a trail of unfinished projects where every they go. In short—this generation, in large, lack the grit to finish and follow through.

Many today are quick to sign up for big dreams, but when the luster of the dream starts to fade and hard work and elbow grease is demanded, they flit off to the next big idea. One, by one, a generation quietly exits the scene, looking for the next hot business idea, the next event, the next adrenaline rush, the next big adventure that might excite them. Their lives fill up with half-finished projects but no trophies. They tinker. They wear their half-finished projects as badges, as a mark of pride as if to show they are created for something greater still. "Oh yeah," they remark, "I started this project here, but then I realized I was really called to this other project, and then I had some dream and I figured out that this other place was really where I was suppose to be . . . " (until the infatuation lifts). "So now I'm waiting for my big break. . . it has been a wild ride, man."

Yes, we need to be flexible and know when to cut our losses. It is best, however, to see commitments and seasons through before jumping into new seasons and commitments.

Apart from being addicted to adrenaline, another snare that keeps us from following through on commitments is the "Fear Of Missing Out," known to some as "FOMO." FOMO, in its most basic form, is merely a strain of comparison. This is a dangerous disease that has spread exponentially thanks to Facebook, Instagram, and so on. How does it spread? I'm sure you know.

You finally land that dream job. Life couldn't be better. Until around four months in . . . your boss isn't as awesome as you thought she might be. Your co-workers aren't as cool. The work is hard... Then it happens. You hear of a *new* position opening up at a different company. A better company. They do cooler work, and the boss is awesome, and the people are cool.

At this point you have a choice. You can put your head down and plow ahead for the next ten years, laboring to see your dreams come true, or you can plan your escape, check out, and make the preparations to jump to the other ship as soon as possible.

The thing is, if you do transfer, your high expectations will not be met. You won't be any cooler, and within a few months, a new thing will pop up that is even better yet. You will find a way to justify this new shift as well, but in reality, you will merely be perpetuating the deathly FOMO cycle.

There is great power in finishing. There is great satisfaction, though fleeting, when we accomplish something great or small. Each time we keep a commitment, following through to the end, we gain momentum. Our word becomes more powerful, our reputation grows, and our confidence builds. We begin to believe we are able to finish what we start.

Conversely, each commitment we break burdens us, causing us to lose momentum. Our word becomes worthless, our reputation erodes, and despair begins to grow like black mold in the hidden recesses of our hearts. We begin to believe the lie that we are powerless and will never amount to anything, because we lack the strength to finish what we start. If we nurture this destructive habit of breaking our word and lack the character to follow through, we will become like a "sluggard [who] buries his hand in the dish and will not even bring it back to his mouth"[27]. Lacking follow-though will land us in spiritual, relational, and economic poverty.

When we adhere to a value within ourselves that declares we will follow through on our word, we begin to handle our word carefully. If we adhere to a value that gives permission to back out of commitments, we will use our words flippantly. Knowing we will follow through and pay the full cost of our word causes us to treat our word with care and value. We will think twice before we speak, and when we do speak our words will carry credibility. There is an ancient proverb that says, "It is a snare to say rashly, It is holy, and to reflect only after making vows."[28] We need to weigh the commitment and the cost before setting out, for if we set out, we must finish. If we do, people will honor, value, and respect our word, and God will entrust us with much.

Give your energy and focus to what is in front of you and where you have given your word. If you put energy in you will get fruit, life, and enjoyment out of where you are today.

Finish what you start. If that means making smaller commitments to test out if you want to follow though on something bigger, then so be it. Guard your word. Be slow to give your word. Once you do give your word, put your head down and don't compare. Finish the task at hand, for there is reward in finishing.

Tools

1) Identify two or three items you started but have failed to finish.
   a. Delineate between activates that were fruitless busywork, which fell to the wayside, and important significant tasks that you lacked the gusto to finish.
   b. If you walked away from it because of lack of grit—man-up, or woman-up, and complete that task.
   c. But, if you abandoned a project because you determined it wasn't a fruitful activity then kill it. Strike it off your list, don't leave it as an unfinished to-do, or another thing you "probably should finish".
2) Set small commitments to build momentum in your life. Think tiny. Start with tasks that can be started, and completed, in a day or a week. No longer.
   a. Don't start committing to large challenges until you first master the smaller ones. This will build your confidence and resolve to finish what you start.

Acknowledgments

I must first thank my strong and incredible wife, Rachael. You encouraged me when I was down, pushed me to write when I was lazy, and created time and space for me to create—all while you yourself were building your own business, and raising four boys. Thank you for believing in me. And thank you for choosing to walk with me on this crazy, and sometimes stupid, path we follow.

Thank you Kevin Miller, my editor and pruner. When I sent you my first draft I knew that my writing was dull and monotonously repetitive. You were honest enough to tell me where it was weak—and then you told me how to fix it. Thank you.

Finally—Thank you Jesus Christ for leading me into one of the most challenging season of my life in order to free me from anxiety and needless busyness.

ANCHORED

About the Author

If you have read this book, you will have a good idea of who Lucas is by now, but if you are flipping through the pages before you buy, or read, the book—here is a little about him:

Lucas Skrobot is an experienced author, speaker, podcaster, and communication strategist. He is recognized for diving deep into people's stories in order to pull out insights, meaning, and purpose that lay hidden in people's lives and narratives.

Through this gifting, he is able to help individuals, brands, and organizations even better understand their identity, empowering them to communicate and serve their audience with excellence.

He has trained and equipped over a thousand freelancers, creatives, entrepreneurs and small business owners in branding, communication, and content strategy.

Go to www.LucasSkrobot.com for more info on how to own your future today.

Speaking Opportunities

Interested in bringing even more clarity to your organization through empowering your members with a greater sense of purpose, meaning, and responsibility to take action?

Lucas delivers talks about purpose, meaning, and action as a path to organizational health and a competitive advantage in your niche. He is the #1 choice if you are looking for a speaker to talk about how the power of story, purpose, and action is needed to lead your organization into the future.

Top reasons why Lucas is the perfect fit for your event

FOR THE AUDIENCE

Lucas' talks are described as, "engaging, deep, and inspiring" giving people a greater clarity in their life, and an even clearer vision of the world.

Relatable:
Given his 11+ years of experience in training, public speaking and communication consulting, he has worked with businesses, educational institutes, universities, entrepreneurs, creatives, freelancers, NGOs, and corporate executives. Audiences are able to bond with his stories and connect to the substance and depth of his experiences.

Engaging:
Lucas is animated, and always engages the audiences through participation. His story driven approach captivates the attention of the audience as he leads them on a journey of exploring new ideas, and opening hearts and minds to their purpose.

Actionable:
Your audience will walk away with action steps. Lucas believes mere listening doesn't bring transformation, rather action and follow through. Lucas is always activating his audience to take-action.

FOR THE EVENT ORGANIZER:

Over the last 11 years, Lucas has spoken at conferences and events across 13 nations and 19 of the 50 United States of America.

Here to Serve:
Lucas comes to serve you, to deliverer to your audience what you desire to give them. Other speakers give hour sales pitches for their services and call them "keynotes". But Lucas always orientates his talks to serve what you, the organizer, needs.

Organized and Flexible:
After hundreds of events, Lucas has learned one thing: Come prepared for the unexpected. He has been in positions where a one-hour key note was cut into 15 minutes, and 20-minute slots was requested to be an hour at the last moment. Lucas come prepared to adapt and serve your needs.

Anti-Pre-Madonna
Lucas knows the stress of organizing, hosting, and running events. Managing talent can be a daunting task. Lucas

doesn't make wild requests or demands. He comes early, stays late—and engages with as many people in the audience as possible.

To sum it up—Lucas comes to serve your needs, your event, and your audience. He isn't seeking to be served.

For more info on booking Lucas for a speaking engagement, get in touch with him directly at Lucas@LucasSkrobot.com

Establish Your Message

Are you seeking to identity, clarify, and communicate your purpose and message in a way that is meaningful to your prospective audience?

You are excellent at your craft after years of discipline and development—now is the time to share your message, connect to your audience, and activate your tribe to reach your collective goal in shaping the world around you.

We help you realize and communicate your core messaging through brand and content strategy and execution— empowering you to define the culture of your organization and build a red-hot activated tribe.

If you are a Profession Expert
(Executive, Entrepreneur, Speaker), Purpose Driven Brand, or
Change Making Organization
we help you
build an activated tribe
by working with you to
clarify your message, communicate your story, and create transformational ecosystems.

Notes

[1] Johansson, Emil "How far and for how many days Frodo travelled in each book," LOTR Project, May 31, 2014. Accessed February 7, 2016, http://lotrproject.com/blog/2014/05/31/how-far-and-for-how-many-days-frodo-travelled-in-each-book/

[2] Kamb, Steve, "How to Walk to Mordor," Nerd Fitness, July 23, 2012. accessed February 7, 2016, http://www.nerdfitness.com/blog/2012/07/23/walking/

[3] "Time Line," LordofRings.com, accessed February 7, 2016, http://www.lordotrings.com/books/timeline.asp

[4] Proverbs 29:18
[5] Proverbs 14:23

[6] Alfie Kohn "Studies Find Reward Often No Motivator," Boston Globe Monday 1987-01-19

[7] Knowles, Brian; "The Hebraic Mindset," Godward.org, Accessed February 7, 2016 http://www.godward.org/hebrew%20roots/hebrew_mind_vs__the_western_mind.htm

[8] Brett and Kate McKay, "What's Your 20 Mile March?" artofmanliness.com, January 6, 2013. Accessed November 30, 2015, http://www.artofmanliness.com/2013/01/06/whats-your-20-mile-march/

[9] Cook, Daniel, "Rules of Productivity" Lostgarden.com, September 28th, 2008. Accessed Feb 7, 2016, http://lunar.lostgarden.com/Rules%20of%20Productivity.pdf

[10] Cook, Daniel, "Rules of Productivity Presentation" Lostgarden.com, September 28th, 2008. Accessed Feb 7, 2016, http://www.lostgarden.com/2008/09/rules-of-productivity-presentation.html

[11] "Napping" National Sleep Foundation. Accessed February 7, 2016 http://sleepfoundation.org/sleep-topics/napping/page/0%2C1/

[12] Van Dongen HP, Mullington JM, Dinges DF. "The cumulative cost of additional wakefulness: dose-response effects on neurobehavioral functions and sleep physiology from chronic sleep restriction and total sleep deprivation." June 15, 2004. Accessed February 7, 2016, http://www.ncbi.nlm.nih.gov/pubmed/12683469

[13] Greenfield, Ben, "The Last Resource You'll Ever Need To Get Better Sleep, Eliminate Insomnia, Beat Jet Lag and Master The Nap: Part 1" bengreenfieldfitness.com, Accessed February 7, 2016, http://www.bengreenfieldfitness.com/2013/07/get-better-sleep/

[14] June J. Pilcher, Allen Huffcutt, "Effects of sleep deprivation on performance: A meta-analysis." *Sleep: Journal of Sleep Research & Sleep Medicine, Vol 19(4),* May 1996, 318–326.

[15] Milne, Sarah; Orbell, Sheina; Sheeran, Paschal, "Combining motivational and volitional interventions to promote exercise participation: Protection motivation theory and implementation intentions" British Journal of Health Psychology Vol 7, Issue 2, Blackwell Publishing Ltd. 2002 , Accessed February 7, 2016, http://dx.doi.org/10.1348/135910702169420

[16] Many books have been written about the 80/20 rule over the past decade and how we can apply it to daily living, business, economics, and so on. *The Four-Hour Work Week* by Tim Ferres and *The 80/20 Principle* by Richard Koch are two of the best-known books on the topic.

[17] M. E. J. Newman, "Power laws, Pareto distributions and Zipf's law," arxiv.org,

http://arxiv.org/PS_cache/cond-mat/pdf/04
z12/0412004v3.pdf (accessed November 30, 2015).

[18] The 10,000 hours rule, originally developed by Anders Ericsson but coined by Malcolm Gladwell in his well-known book, "The Outliers", basically states that it requires 10,000 hours of deliberate work and practice to become an extraordinary expert in any one field.

[19] Brailsford, Dave, "'Marginal Gains' Interview with Dave Brailsford GB Cycling Performance Director " Youtube, October 29, 2012. Accessed February 7, 2016, http://www.youtube.com/watch?v=gBY3q8TqoXY

[20] Gado, Mark (November 2008). "The Kitty Genovese Murder". *TruTV*. Archived from the original on March 22, 2013.

[21] Darley, J. M. & Latané, B. (1968). Bystander intervention in emergencies: diffusion of responsibility. Journal of Personality and Social Psychology, 8, 377-383.

[22] Ellison Harlon (1983). "100: March 26, 71". *The Other Glass Teat*. New York: Ace Books. p. 383 ISBN 978-0-44164-274-8

[23] Ciccarelli, S. K. & White, J. N. (2009). Psychology (2nd ed.) New Jersey: Pearson Education. ISBN 978-0-13-600428-8.

[24] Kassin Fein; Markus Burke (2013). Social Psychology. Toronto: Nelson Education.

[25] Ciccarelli, S. K. & White, J. N. (2009). Psychology (2nd ed.) New Jersey: Pearson Education. ISBN 978-0-13-600428-8.

[26] Psalm 75:7; Daniel 2:21

[27] Proverbs 19:24
[28] Proverbs 20:25